THE FRENCH TOUCH

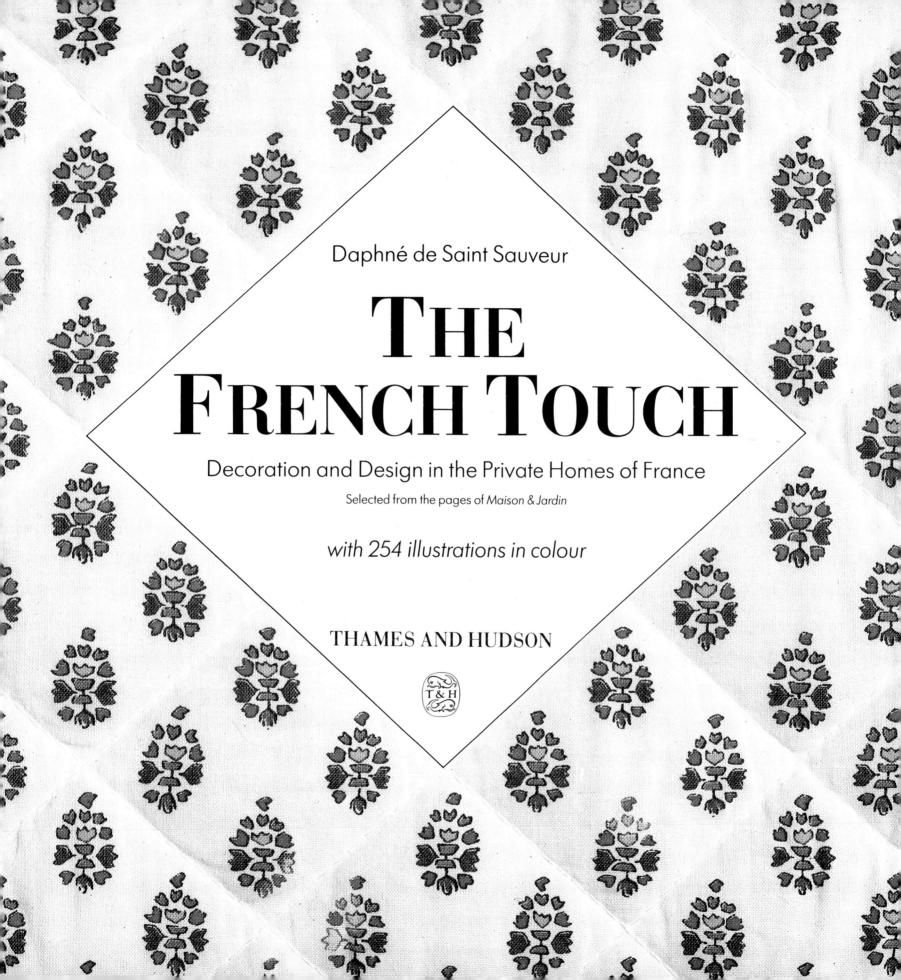

Daphné de Saint Sauveur

THE FRENCH TOUCH

Decoration and Design in the Private Homes of France

Selected from the pages of *Maison & Jardin*

with 254 illustrations in colour

THAMES AND HUDSON

On the title page:
Country mood, Paris style, by the designer Martine Nourissat.

Translated from the French by Emily Lane

Printed and bound in Italy

CONTENTS

INTRODUCTION

Another book on interior design? My shelves are already filled with them and overflowing. No doubt yours are too . . . Books on modernizing a Tudor cottage or transforming a loft into an apartment; on how to live in a cave; on reviving Sixties style; on covering your bedroom in fabric and your kitchen in wood; on rehabilitating an African hut, converting a Greek fisherman's cottage or restoring a manor house in Brittany; on redesigning everything from the bathroom to the broom closet . . . There is no end to them. Dozens of such books come out every year, each in its own way treating that apparently inexhaustible subject, interior decoration.

"Once more, with feeling," says the song. So here is my contribution, or I should say ours, since it is based on the work of the *Maison & Jardin* team. Rather like a guidebook, it invites you to wander through the landscape of design in town and countryside. To be precise, it invites you into thirty-five apartments and houses in Paris, the Ile de France, the West, the South-West, and the South, where you will find thirty-five different kinds of French design: simple, as in a farm in Normandy rescued by a painter in love with genuine country life; grandiloquent, as in a perfectly proportioned Parisian apartment; sophisticated, as in another apartment where the crimson curtains suggest the sultry, sinister world of Barbey d'Aurevilly but also the gaiety of a box at a Verdi opera; welcoming, as in a former silk farm in Provence transformed into a vacation house; classical, as in a villa near Toulouse decorated in late 19th-century style; engaging, as in the wing of a chateau in the Bordeaux region which has been altered and revitalized by a new generation of owners. Thirty-five places chosen among many to illustrate a certain kind of taste, what Chateaubriand called "the good sense of genius."

A summer house on the banks of the Marne, redolent of the sweetness of France. It belonged to Victor Laloux, architect of the Gare d'Orsay in Paris at the turn of the century; the designer Gérard Franc has preserved its old-fashioned charm.

Let us be modest in our claims, however: this is of course not a comprehensive survey of every possible sort of French style. There are thousands of fine old houses whose architecture and furnishings survive more or less untouched as witnesses of the past – at Barbentane near Avignon, for instance, Montgeoffroy near Tours, Jussy near Bourges – not to mention the great chateaux, more or less well-known, that figure on tourist itineraries and would need a score of books to do them justice. Interesting, magnificent, and French they may be, but this book is not about them: it is concerned with contemporary trends in interior design.

Personality counts now rather than safe traditional styles; originality rather than mere opulence; imagination rather than convention; and comfort rather than display. Even if they sometimes seem to include references to the past, the homes that you will see were designed to be lived in today; and they are full of ideas that can easily be adapted. Above all, they have been chosen for their charm – that seductive quality, as irresistible as it is intangible, independent of time and passing fashions, that blooms in any home, small or large, in the city or the depths of the country, that has been furnished with love.

What is charm? How can we pin it down? Is it due to a well-thought-out plan? a particular color harmony? a poetic atmosphere? a chair that welcomes you, a painting that enchants you, a "find" that fills you with excitement, a bouquet of flowers that offers itself to you? Is it explained by that love of balance, of the *juste milieu*, for which we French are famous? Or is there something in it of frivolity, for which we are equally well-known? Could it be that a certain logical, acerbic Gallic wit underlies the creation of a successful interior? Hard to say. But what does seem certain is that it depends on a whole host of varied details and that it raises domesticity to the level of art. And surely charm is what characterizes a French interior, just as timeless good taste characterizes the classic English house, cheerful comfort the American, aesthetic rigor the Italian, sumptuous austerity the Spanish, and intelligent functionalism the homes of Scandinavia.

Houses resemble their inhabitants. Discreetly or flamboyantly, they express their aspirations and their behavior – one person's dreams of nobility, another's bourgeois common sense, the humor of a third, the grandiose ambition of a fourth. You can learn more about people's manners and customs from their homes than from any number of social and sociological surveys. In France conversation is, if not

8

a substitute for sport, at least a favorite pastime. And the place where family and friends gather – the informal *petit salon* or sitting room, the living room, the *grand salon* or drawing room – is the heart of the house. Here you will find the finest pieces of furniture, the best pictures and *objets d'art*, and the softest carpets; here the owner will hang the newest curtains, place the most fashionable sofas, and give most care to the lighting. It is the room most loved by designers and by the mistress of the house, and its decoration sets the tone for everything else. Next comes the dining room, as you would expect in a country where gastronomy is almost a religion. As much care goes into its arrangement as into the preparation of a cordon bleu meal: with its display of dishes on the walls, its candelabra and silverware, its plates and glasses chosen with exquisite care, the table itself a masterpiece of composition, the room feasts the eye before it feasts the palate. And the bedroom? According to our reputation abroad, this ought to be the most important room of all. The canopied beds, pretty printed fabrics, gauzy muslins and delicate furniture should perfectly convey that mood of sophistication and seduction that is, rightly or wrongly, considered to be so very French. Do they match your ideas? It is for you to say. And you must decide, too, whether these thirty-five houses and apartments chosen from the pages of *Maison & Jardin* conform to your idea of the "French touch." For me, each of these places represents one facet of the beloved land of my childhood. Each room displays the talent of architects, interior designers, craftsmen, colorists and others whose taste is matched only by their perfectionism. Not *all* the available talent, though: once again, let us be modest in our claims. To cover new trends not yet part of the mainstream, and to examine ideas that may form the creative world of tomorrow, would require a second volume. Another book on interior design?

My shelves are overflowing. Yours too, perhaps . . .

1

PARIS: THE DECORATOR'S EYE

They are the ones who set the tone, start new fashions, create color harmonies, invent mixtures of styles, manage space; they who, by their skill, coax out the personality of a house. "They" are interior designers. That is to say technicians, colorists, researchers, artists, poets, psychologists – and more. Without their imagination, our bourgeois apartment in town would look just like that of our great-aunt, and our country house would be merely rural; eternal safe beige would still be our favorite color, 18th-century furniture (genuine or fake) would be the touchstone of good taste, and bedrooms would still be bowers of flowered chintz. These "pros" lay before us a treasure-chest of ideas. They let us share their aesthetic sense and their skill. They encourage us to be bold, but also sensible: together with clever conceits and ingenious tricks, they give us lessons in taste. One teaches us how to hang pictures; another how to group objects into compositions; a third how to use fabrics; a fourth how to arrange happy marriages between unlikely partners. Some give detailed information on sophisticated improvements to a bathroom or how to transform a dressing-room into a kitchen. So when Madeleine Castaing, Jacques Grange, Sabine Imbert, Dominique Menvielle-Bourg and other Parisian interior designers ask us in, we should rush to take up their invitation. It is fitting that they should also usher us into this book.

Favorite books and *objets* in the apartment of the designer
Dominique Menvielle-Bourg (see p. 28).

AUTUMN FIRES

Some designers find inspiration for a decorative scheme in a painting, the pattern of a carpet, or the colors in some exotic fabric brought back from abroad. For others it might be the motif on a plate, or a collection of objects, prints or china. Yet others take their cue from the style of the building or the view from a window. For Michèle Gayraud, who has worked closely with Jacques Grange and is a designer in her own right, the spark was a bunch of autumn leaves picked up in the park at St.-Cloud. Faded green, dark red, and all shades from yellow through to brown give her apartment a golden autumnal glow. There are comfortable large sofas, books within easy reach, well-placed lamps, and eloquent groups of objects; and there is, too, a remarkable spaciousness, as the doors between the rooms stand open. It all feels rather like a formal French garden. Might that, too, have been inspired by an autumn walk?

Skilfully composed still-lifes enliven a chest of drawers and a fireplace. To a mixture of bronzes and Gallé glass vases (*above*) Michèle Gayraud has added two little paintings, treated as if they were *objets d'art. Opposite:* Amusing 19th-century ceramics stand below a painting from Cuzco in Peru, which is hung against the mirror. The objects pick up the main colors used in the apartment.

Above: A detail of the library fireplace. Another painting from Cuzco is hung against the mirror; below it is a 19th-century bust garlanded with an antique tasseled cord.

Left: A view of the living room, with the library beyond. The doors are almost always left open, but they can be partly or wholly closed like the panels of a screen. The use of the same patinated yellow tone for the sponged walls in both rooms gives a sense of space and continuity. In the foreground is a big, low Chinese table. On either side of the door are paintings by Mucha, framed in simple strips of wood.

Let's be flexible! The library, lined with limed oak shelves, contains an English mahogany table that normally serves, soberly skirted, as a reading desk. At mealtimes, however, the cloth is removed, places are laid, and you are in a dining room. Instead of curtains, fine wooden blinds let in a golden light.

A STAGE SET
FOR LIVING

"Without red, life wouldn't be the same" – that was the message of a brand of whisky that made a feature of its red label. And certainly without red the apartment of the Parisian coiffeur Alexandre Zouari would be very different. It would not be so theatrical, so festive, such a brilliant stage for innumerable objects. But happily the red was chosen, and the stage brilliantly set, by Madeleine Castaing, who has been the unchallenged diva of French interior design since the war. How does she set about it? "When you design a house for somebody else you have to feel an affinity for them, because you must enter wholeheartedly into their private life." Her rapport with Alexandre Zouari was complete, and the harmony between her literary tastes ("Balzac is a source of inspiration that can be followed word for word," she says) and his love of antiques was ideal. The outcome is like a series of numbers from an opera – a duet between red walls and mahogany, a trio consisting of furniture from 19th-century England, Second Empire France and Biedermeier Austria. Curtain! Bravissimo!

The living room end of the main room, which is divided into three zones. Furniture and objects of the 19th century from England, France and Austria are set off by the walls hung with red felt.

The dining area (*above*) feels like a box at the opera a hundred years ago. The Russian candelabra and Austrian chairs give this intimate space a Central European flavor. A view of the other end of the same room (*opposite*) is framed by a pair of English wooden urns. Note the careful hanging of the pictures and the extra-wide braid that divides the walls up into panels.

SLEEPING BEAUTY AWAKENED

The story of this house is like the tale of Sleeping Beauty. It was built at the beginning of this century for the Princesse de Polignac (Winnie Singer, the sewing machine heiress); a famous patron and hostess, she held dazzling receptions for her literary and musical friends, among them Marcel Proust, Paul Valéry, Anna de Noailles, Maurice Ravel and Gabriel Fauré. Then it slept for thirty years in dust and oblivion, a reality only in the memory of those who had known it. Not long ago the designer Sylvie Nègre, wizard-like, broke the slumbrous spell and it awoke in beauty. The chief task was to restore the delicate paintings on the walls and to recapture the original feeling while providing the comforts of modern living. After months of meticulous work, and new decoration sensitive to the spirit of the place, the Princesse de Polignac's house is starting out on a new life.

A special feature of the house is the decorative paintings in Directoire style on the walls. Furnishings and colors in the circular salon are deliberately reticent: white sofas, a low table of travertine and limed wood, cabriolet chairs, and light silk curtains modestly allow the room itself to play the starring role.

The bathroom is on the mezzanine level that Sylvie Nègre tucked
into the great room. One of the original overdoors, protected by
glass, was reset on the wall behind the splendid old-fashioned
bathtub.

Top: The walls of the entrance hall are treated to look like stone,
and the floor is paved with stone from Nancy. *Above:* The library
with its oak bookcases can also serve as a dining room. Sylvie Nègre
used slipcovers of printed fabric to cheer up the chairs.

25

To make the grand room used as a bedroom less awesome, Sylvie Nègre introduced a mezzanine big enough to hold bookshelves and a desk (*above*). The stairs leading up to it, designed with a nod to Directoire forms, also have the effect of creating an alcove for the bed.

INFINITE WHITENESS IN A LITTLE ROOM

What is it that in everyday life can be cold, like snow, boring, like milk, empty, like the page of a writer who can't think how to begin? White. What is it in design that unifies an interior, makes it seem more spacious, creates super-simple chic and elegance? White again. The apartment of Dominique Menvielle-Bourg, a designer attached to the Galerie Maison et Jardin, is the perfect proof of this paradoxical fact. In what is basically a single room in Montmartre, all shades of white blend happily together, the wood of the furniture and the natural materials of handmade pottery and basketwork stand out to perfection, and sobriety itself seems warm. What is it in these skilfully arranged spaces that is immediately striking and completely enchanting? White, absolutely.

White well-used in a city apartment – in the slipcover of the sofa, the chalky walls, the carpet which is almost rustic, and the painting by Lionel Godart. All this whiteness is offset by the wood of the antique Provençal chair and the two Chinese endtables. The same game of counterpoint is played in the bathroom (right foreground), where a birdcage is placed against pure white walls.

Right: The living room has a Mediterranean look. The shelving is of stone and wood painted white; and the table with its travertine top and foot separated by a column of altuglass and the white-painted folding stools look as though they had been brought in from a terrace.

Looking through the full length of the apartment from the bedroom to the living room (*left*), the view is like a graphic design, incorporating the eloquent shapes of an almost Oriental-looking gondola prow and of the living room furniture and objects silhouetted against the window. Note how the bedhead is a box, concealing stereo equipment.

The bedroom itself (*opposite*) has a strong Japanese, Zen, feeling, though one isn't quite sure why: is it the bed, placed simply on a rectangular base covered with woven wooden strips; the tester, also of woven wooden strips, suspended overhead on two poles of natural wood; the bamboo chair, that looks like an ideogram; the woodcut-like composition of objects and plant against Oriental-style blinds; or the overall serenity? There is also an ingenious touch of Western elegance: shelves and closets are concealed behind linen drapes.

A WELL-ORDERED WORLD

Personality sometimes derives from the ordering of things. Imagine this apartment without its objects: it would be light, spacious, and no doubt pleasant to live in, but it would be ordinary – just like any of thousands of other Parisian apartments. Introduce masses of books, fin de siècle *paintings and amusing antiques, a few pieces of country furniture, old-fashioned chairs, a piano, a cat, a dog, and the taste of an inveterate hunter among junk shops. The result is a unique environment, with the timeless charm that is the hallmark of the antique dealer and designer Anne Gayet.*

White-painted shelves frame the bedroom door
(*right*) and a view through to the living room.
On the piano (*above*) is a little grouping of
objects that include snuff boxes shaped like cats
and a painting by Marie Bashkirtseff.

The summery bedroom suggests a Mediterranean siesta even in the depths of wintry Paris. The bedcover and drapes are of white linen, as is the slipcover on the armchair. The mosquito net hung above the bed gives an unexpected and delicious exotic touch.

In the living room, pale walls, ceiling and woodwork set off the furniture and objects, whose apparent disorder is carefully studied – in the foreground, a display of tobacco holders in the form of wooden shoes, and elsewhere small antiques grouped by themes.

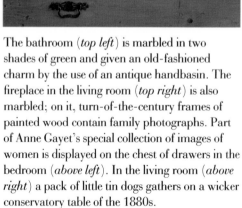

The bathroom (*top left*) is marbled in two shades of green and given an old-fashioned charm by the use of an antique handbasin. The fireplace in the living room (*top right*) is also marbled; on it, turn-of-the-century frames of painted wood contain family photographs. Part of Anne Gayet's special collection of images of women is displayed on the chest of drawers in the bedroom (*above left*). In the living room (*above right*) a pack of little tin dogs gathers on a wicker conservatory table of the 1880s.

Opposite: The dining room feels a bit like the country. The 18th-century Alsatian dresser holds another of Anne Gayet's collections, of pottery jugs made around 1900. The table is covered with a quilt and surrounded by 19th-century bamboo café chairs. As in the other rooms, fine Venetian blinds filter the light and provide privacy from neighbors' eyes.

THE PAST IN THE PRESENT TENSE

Can you make a sentence in the present tense out of statements in the past? Indeed you can. To give it a special eloquence, the owner of this house in Paris called upon the skills of two designers, Vincent Fourcade and François Catroux, who each interpreted her ideas in his own way. Thus it is that an 18th-century interior is the setting for a happy composition of furniture and objects ranging in period from Louis XV through Louis XVI, Directoire, Empire, Charles X and Louis-Philippe to Napoleon III. It is timeless – but also, most importantly, perfectly adapted to the life of today.*

Above: The living room. There are Louis XVI candlesticks on a Louis XV table, an English stool serving as a low table, a Charles X clock on the Louis XVI mantelpiece, and comfortable modern sofas. A large Aubusson carpet draws it all together.

Opposite: The dining room, lit by candles in an Empire chandelier and wall sconces, has a painted ceiling that is listed on the register of historic monuments. The embroidered upholstery of the Louis-Philippe chairs is a stitch-for-stitch copy of the original design.

A living room on the upper floor in Proustian mood, with a central circular ottoman topped with the traditional potted palm. Note the marbling and wood-graining on the door.

A 19th-century lantern hangs over the stairs; an antique bathtub from the Marché aux Puces, filled with plants, brightens the landing.

'PLAINE MONCEAU' STYLE

Sabine Marchal belongs to that new generation of Parisian women designers who bring a little extra something to their work – practical common sense? a feminine way of seeing? could one simply call it charm? Charm is certainly the quality she has imparted to the house in the Plaine Monceau district of which the ground floor is occupied by the art gallery of her husband, Didier Imbert: one glance at her transformation of its formal rooms is proof enough. With a few pretty fabrics and carpets in carefully chosen colors, a little furniture and a lot of ideas, she has made a somewhat grandiloquent Second Empire house into a cheerful setting for family life with four children.

In the dining room (*above*) the paneling was stripped to provide a background for drawings by Salvador Dali and silver from Puiforcat. What had been a dressing room became a kitchen (*left*). The painted woodwork was retained, together with the closets, which now hold dishes, but the modern world has been welcomed in – a television, for instance, is set into the counter dividing the room.

Opposite: The main staircase leading up to the private apartments is imposing, but its serious tone is lightened by Italianate games played with *trompe-l'oeil* painting and mirrors.

On a Louis XVI commode, a tablescape of decorative Chinese blue-and-white porcelain picks up colors in the painting and in the swirly Paisley pattern wall covering.

Points to note in the living room, that looks out over the Parc Monceau, are the exquisite drapes and Austrian blinds of lightweight silk and the wall-to-wall carpet designed to harmonize with the wall covering. A fabric-covered ottoman in the center serves as a table and provides storage space.

In the master bedroom (*left*) the bed is concealed by a triple-frilled skirt, but the lace and embroidered linen pillowcases are left exposed. The bathroom that opens off this bedroom (*opposite*) is linked to it visually by the same patterned wall covering and carpet. Two clever ideas: the two-tone cord used instead of the conventional braid where the wall covering meets the cornice and baseboard, and the mahogany paneling that gives the bathtub/jacuzzi a traditional, 'boudoir' feeling.

The guest bedroom and *en suite* bathroom were designed to form a little self-contained apartment. The bedhead is covered with a Paisley fabric that matches the walls of the bathroom. The amusing two-part mirror over the handbasin comes from the Marché aux Puces.

LUXURIOUS
SOBRIETY

There are meetings that are too perfect to be accidental. When the apartment of one of the greatest French writers of the 20th century fell vacant, it seemed almost inevitable for it to be taken by the most brilliant French designer. So it is that Jacques Grange now occupies the apartment of Colette, looking out over the gardens of the Palais Royal. Here, under the eye of her vivacious ghost, he established what he describes as a man's apartment, "rigorous, classical and French." Let us wander through this unique, inimitable interior. Those who know Jacques Grange's work will recognize his love of books and old photographs, his admiration for Jean-Michel Frank and Matisse, his subtle daring when it comes to the juxtaposition of objects, his refusal to conform to fashion, his fondness for muted colors, his utter contempt for flashy effects, and his perfectionism when it comes to detailing and quality. Those unfamiliar with Grange will discover exquisitely elegant rooms pervaded by a sense of poetry but also a sense of humor. They will above all be impressed by the complete sobriety. Is this really the home of the man responsible for so many prestigious installations, for clients ranging from Yves Saint Laurent to Lloyds? If, as Chanel said, luxury is the opposite of vulgarity, then this is perfect luxury. And, what is more, it makes one want to move in at once, and live in the Palais Royal, in the realm of Jacques Grange . . .

The dining room, with its pair of French doors leading into the study/ library, gives a first glimpse of Jacques Grange's eclectic taste: pinkish ochre walls, embroidered carpet from Bokhara, 19th-century Russian folding screen, painting by Louise Abbema, and 19th-century Japanese baskets.

The famous Jacques Grange style is displayed in its most perfect form in the living room. A Neo-Gothic screen provides a background for a sofa and a table by Emilio Terri. In front of the sofa, a table by Dunand is flanked by two Art Deco armchairs. On the far wall, in the library, are some of the designer's beloved photographs, which include portraits of Baudelaire, George Sand and Victor Hugo. On the mantelpiece (*above*) is a bust by Gimond; this corner of the room is simple in its arrangement and muted in color – but the windows look out on the green world of the Palais Royal gardens.

Left and below: An iron bedstead of delicately graphic silhouette sets the tone of this bedroom. Graphic too are the stripes of the wallpaper, the Neo-Gothic bench in front of the fireplace, and the arrangement of the pictures whose gold frames harmonize with the autumnal coloring of the room.

A guest bedroom,
decorated as for the
master of the chateau's
daughter, is almost
filled by a Louis XV
canopied bedstead.

The centrally positioned library is the first room you enter in the apartment. Notice the contrasting character of the angular slate desk, the unusual chair, and the simple wooden bookshelves.

A characteristic
grouping of objects and
mementos on the
mantelpiece in one of
the bedrooms:
simplicity, wit and taste
come together to create
a perfect still-life.

2

PARIS: THE PERSONAL TOUCH

One apartment occupies the vast piano nobile *of an early 17th-century house such as you find in the Marais. Two others are charmingly set in the attic stories of old buildings. Yet another is, quite extraordinarily, fitted into the ballroom of a former mansion in one of the rich quarters of the city. The rest are luxury apartments with classic proportions typical of the late 19th century. Different locations, different types of dwelling . . . But all these apartments, decorated by their owners with greater or less means and with an abundance of ideas, have one thing in common: a passionate, mad, overwhelming love of objects in great numbers. Presented as collections, grouped into still-lifes, arranged in compositions, isolated like punctuation marks, rare pieces or unusual knick-knacks, trifles bought for a few pennies or extraordinary discoveries, they give each of these homes its individual look and, in the end, its personality. In fashion, as we know, the line of a garment is the deciding factor, but it is the choice of accessories which makes all the difference and supplies the element of chic. In decoration, arrangement is important and harmony essential, but it is the details which actually set the tone; and, when you look closely at these examples of Paris homes, the details create what one is tempted to call "the style of the capital."*

Food for mind and body in a Parisian library-cum-dining room.

THE COLORS
OF HAPPINESS

Manuel Canovas has style. Designing the fabrics for which he is famous or sketching flowers for his own delight, talking about his latest travels in Asia or his collection of 18th-century drawings, describing the various kinds of sand that he brings back from all over the world or making up a bouquet of old roses, he does everything with a mixture of originality, chic, wit and imagination that is uniquely his. And his style naturally pervades the stately apartment into which he recently moved with his wife and children, where he has redesigned everything with dash and skill. The hall off which most of the rooms open is treated like a hunting lodge, the drawing room suggests an ancestral home, the master bedroom has an English freshness, and the dining room might be in an Italian palazzo – and over everything, in all these rooms, Manuel Canovas has spread the colors of happiness.

58

In the sitting room, a chintz patterned with lavish peonies in blue-and-white china vases sets off the paintings and 19th-century portraits, among them a large watercolor by Isabelle de Borchgrave above the console table. Two small, refined details, not be missed, are the ball of dried rosebuds on a curtain tieback, and the Chinese teapot that inspired the design of the fabric.

The entrance hall/library. The geometrical pattern of the carpet, the stripes of the Austrian blind, and the flowers on the walls harmonize with the golden oak woodwork.

Right: A genuine 18th-century color scheme sings out in the drawing room. Note the clever arrangement of drawings, prints, miniatures and ornaments on the walls, and the seating grouped to form several separate areas.

Candy shades – chiefly mint – color the bedroom, centered on a
great fourposter bed. Seashells and other little mementos are
enclosed in two glass tables.

The dining room, hung with pink moire outlined with *trompe-l'oeil* marble and chalcedony, and ornamented with 17th-century Spanish portraits and antique ceramics and glass, is reminiscent of Italy or of a stage set for a Mozart opera.

OBJECTS ON PARADE

Birgitta Fouret was born in Sweden, began her career as a designer in the United States, has lived for many years in Paris, and stocks her Parisian antique shop in England. How does someone with such an international background react to the French spirit? Her apartment in the 7th arrondissement, cosmopolitan and highly personal, provides the answer. Some of the furniture is Swedish, *"Gustaviansk" or Empire. The carpets are Oriental kilims. The paintings and prints are British or Italian. And the innumerable objects are Scandinavian or English. The architecture, however, is typically French, with its plaster moldings, columns and pilasters. And the very air of Paris, indefinable but unmistakable, does the rest. Isn't that itself a sort of "French touch"?*

In the living room two Moorish warriors of painted bronze guard a herd of 19th-century elephants in ivory and bronze (*above*), while on another table (*opposite*) lions, and ivory and silver magnifying glasses and letter openers, are grouped below an 18th-century watercolor.

Opposite: Birgitta Fouret's office perfectly indicates both her taste and her national origin. Note the Swedish chair in front of the roll-top desk, the pair of English children's armchairs upholstered in Paisley shawls, and the rare collection of objects made of Swedish Alvdalen porphyry on the mantelpiece. Here as elsewhere in the apartment the floor is stained black.

Above: In the study/library, seal impressions, cameos and medals are framed and hung against a background of red fabric — an inventive way of gathering small items together and displaying them to advantage.

In the living room, seats with simple white slipcovers partner
unusual pieces of Swedish 19th-century furniture. Points to note:
the casually positioned throws of antique striped silk, and the simple
Scandinavian style drapes of lightweight fabric at the windows.

Top: The bedroom is simple and light, but given spice by the pimento red hangings of the fourposter bed and the drapes. A kilim in the same tones is laid over wall-to-wall carpeting, and a bench is silhouetted against the window.

Above: The hall is made to seem longer by repetition of the decorative elements – kilims, Swedish chests of drawers, Karl Johan chairs covered with kilim, and a large collection of engravings from William Cavendish's 17th-century book on horsemanship.

A WANDERING SOUL

This sunny room on the top floor of a Parisian apartment building, stuffed with exotic treasures, looks rather like the home of Marco Polo, back from his long travels in the East. In fact it belongs to someone almost as romantic – an antique dealer turned historical novelist, Sylvie Simon. As a writer, she can bring to life heroines of the past such as Isabella d'Este and the Napoleonic Duchesse d'Abrantès; how alert she must be to the voices of her Chinese, Burmese and Japanese furniture, her Romantic and Pre-Raphaelite paintings, her Far Eastern objets d'art and sculptured busts! These objects crowding in from faraway places and faraway times stand out against the white walls of her apartment as the characters in a book stand out against its white pages. They constitute the decorative grammar of the place – not surprisingly, perhaps, in the home of a writer . . .

The apartment consists essentially of a single large room, from which a flight of steps leads up to a roof terrace. Among the many intriguing objects one might single out four 19th-century busts of colored marble representing the seasons, and a 19th-century Japanese mirror in its original tasseled frame.

Opposite: An 18th-century lacquer box from Burma stands on a Chinese lacquer chest of drawers of the same date. *Above:* Around the piano, itself of a glossy lacquer black, pictures tell tales from three centuries – the 18th, in a scene of a family in the country, the 19th, in an English oil of a galloping horse, and the 20th, in the large Japanese figure painting on panel.
Right: A 19th-century Japanese ironwood chair.

METAMORPHOSIS IN THE MARAIS

Sic transit gloria domus – *the glory of the house is passed away . . .* *This palatial apartment on the main floor of one of the oldest houses in the Marais was in a sorry state when the painter Gaston Berthelot moved in a few years ago. The previous occupants had been a firm of porcelain manufacturers, and the only surviving indications of past grandeur were the proportions of the rooms themselves, and the stone and parquet floors. To attempt a restoration of the original appearance would have been not only expensive but dubious; and so the artist called on his imagination to breathe life back into the shell. On the walls, stripped of their paneling, he used sponged paintwork in three colors taken from a fresco by Tiepolo; to furnish the enfilade of three large rooms, no carpets, just a few pieces of furniture, seats covered with white linen like the summer dust-covers in an Italian palazzo; and to give a feeling of authenticity, antique chandeliers hung in a traditional way. It is a style of decoration that seems improvised, of the sort popular in the 17th century – and the 20th century too.*

This vast room, originally an antechamber, now serves as a studio for Gaston Berthelot, who prefers its warm southern light. The table, a Second Empire copy of one by Cressent, holds paints and brushes grouped together in pots.

The drawing room, illuminated in the afternoon by sun from the garden and in the evening by candles – real and counterfeit – in candlesticks and chandeliers. Note the textured effect of the walls, achieved with colored glazes; the white linen draped casually over the seats; and the sleeves covering the chandelier chains, which match the taffeta drapes.

Left: A view down the enfilade from the studio past the drawing room (formerly a picture gallery) to the bedroom, transformed into a sitting room.

Opposite: The end of the vista: a console table, placed in front of an antique mirror, displays an early 17th-century fountain of Rouen faience and a pair of ducks from Tunisia, where the painter often goes in search of inspiration.

PASTICHE
AND PROFUSION

Some rules in interior design are meant to be broken. Take this apartment: it consists of three small rooms, of which two form the living room while the third is the bedroom. Conventional wisdom would have it that to make this space seem bigger, or at least no smaller, the decorator should play safe with two colors and scarcely more than three pieces of furniture. But Gilles Dufour – a fashion designer, a close colleague of Karl Lagerfeld at Chanel, and a master of proportion – opted for the opposite, choosing for his apartment a lush 19th-century style. Filled with fabrics of different patterns, with an accumulation of objects, and with big old paintings in their original frames, the space takes on a warm and comfortable feeling. Style makes one forget size; originality conceals defects. And that, surely, justifies the sleight-of-hand.

To create an impression of space, don't decrease the colors and the contrasts – increase them. In the living room everything but the plain yellow walls and one sofa is overlaid with pattern: notice the Oriental carpet and kilim laid over matting, the upholstery and curtains in stripes or Paisley swirls, the bookcase crammed with books but also with objects, the many paintings – some of them very large – and the little occasional tables covered with *bibelots* and plants.

The bedroom/study is also furnished with an eye for rich effects. On the walls a striped fabric is combined with wood-graining for the doors and closets. The seat of the chesterfield is covered with an antique patchwork quilt, and the window, hung with striped drapes and a patterned blind, is flanked by library shelves.

SENSE AND SENSITIVITY

Is it the sloping ceilings with their exposed beams? the layout of the rooms, in the attic story of an apartment building? the serene atmosphere? the view of the garden from the windows? Something *about this apartment in the clouds makes it feel like a proper house – a house that combines rural charm and urban elegance. For elegance is the hallmark of Christian Badin's decoration, as he responded to the wishes of the mistress of the house. Is she fond of symmetry? The living room has two matching sets of bookshelves (of which one pair frames the door to the bedroom), and four identical Restauration armchairs surround the sofa. Is she interested in petit-point embroidery? The blue carpet on the living room floor, based on an 18th-century design, was worked by her own hands. Is she sensitive to refined allusions? The bedroom is arranged like a boudoir in an 18th-century print. Does she love blue? Here and there in the luminous rooms are objects of the same forget-met-not blue as her eyes. Isn't that the last word in refinement?*

A tented canopy above the bed, a pretty Paisley pattern slightly tinged with mauve on walls and furniture, and a few exquisite little bits and pieces suffice to transform the bedroom into a boudoir.

Opposite: A bouquet of ranunculus, an antique stoppered bottle of engraved glass, and a touch of the owner's favorite blue create a charming composition on a simple table by the sofa.

The clean white kitchen (occupying the space of several utility rooms), with its collection of blue-and-white plates, has a Scandinavian look.

The living room, fitted into the attic by an ingenious architect. Notice the staircase, half concealed, that leads up to a bathroom tucked in at a slightly higher level, and the original attic window that illuminates a Louis XV writing table.

AFTER THE BALL

*This room once echoed to waltzes and quadrilles: it was the
ballroom of a private house, built out over the garden in the early
years of this century. When the music stopped it became a storeroom,
and then was forgotten. A young antique dealer with a particular
love of unusual and out-of-the-way places recently set up home here,
after doing the bare minimum of alterations in order to squeeze in a
bedroom, kitchen and bathroom. He enlarged the original fountain
and surrounded it with steps, and added two more columns to the
original ones of granite. The effect is of a patio – in Granada, near
the gardens of the Generalife? in the residential district of Beirut?
No: in Paris, in the home of that most hospitable man, Maroun
Salloum. With an array of guests – there is room for ten, or twenty,
of fifty – you can dine beside the pool under the palm trees, listening
to civilized conversation, and imagine yourself a thousand miles
away. With a past like that, what does the future hold?*

Previous pages
In the great room four
potted palms around
the pool stand on
marble steps, which
serve as seats at parties.
On the walls at the back
and behind the table by
Diego Giacometti on the
right are 18th-century
prints depicting battles
fought by the Emperor
Chien Lung. In one
corner a table covered
with a 19th-century
Indian carpet supports
a pyramid of
pomegranates in a
19th-century cooler, a
Chinese vase, and a
"maître d'hôtel cat" by
Diego Giacometti,
backed by a golden
17th-century Japanese
screen.

The owner has an antique dealer's eye for mixing different periods and cultures.
Opposite: A 19th-century Austrian circular table and a Japanese table are seen against two strips of late 18th-century French Chinoiserie wallpaper.
Right: The low table is a 19th-century English folding daybed; on it stands an 18th-century Imari pot. In the background are 19th-century crystal girandoles and 18th-century Italian craftsmen's masterworks.

EVERY OBJECT
TELLS A STORY

"A place for everything, and everything in its place:" that might be the ruling principle of this enlightened art-lover, surrounded by a profusion of diverse and remarkable objects from the past. He collects things for the simple pleasure of looking at them, but best of all he loves the ones that chime with the style of his apartment. He has a particular passion for unusual objects with intriguing histories, such as a chandelier whose miraculous escape from a fire is as important to him as its shape. The fact that a picture frame was made for the Palais Rose in the great days of the dashing Count Boni de Castellane delights him at least as much as its carved and gilded swirls. What if there appears to be no story? Then he does research, even goes so far as to take something to pieces to understand its mysteries. Or, with a bit of trompe l'oeil *paintwork, he invents a past – and at a stroke a future – so that everything tells a story.*

The drawing room walls are covered with strawpaper painted in a shade of pink that enhances the paintings. The curtains of silk doupion are also pink, while the doors are grained, with black moldings. Over the fireplace is a 17th-century French painting between two 18th-century Meissen jars, while on either side Louis XV sconces, bronze plaques and framed panels are arranged symmetrically. Note the little picture on a low easel positioned like a fire guard.

Opposite: Again in the drawing room, symmetry extends to the placing of the two black leather chesterfields. A bust by Houdon, of terracotta finished to look like bronze, stands next to the door leading to the dining room. An English square piano is used as a table to display 16th- and 17th-century bronzes and a cabinetmaker's masterwork.

Right: The sitting room. Among the pictures hung against the 1930s wallpaper is a drawing in red chalk by Boucher.

Above: Delectable deception in the dining room: the table looks like terracotta, the walls seem to be covered with trellising, and you could almost swear the cornice was Wedgwood.

Opposite: In the bedroom, a big American brass bed faces the finest work in the room, Van Loo's *Experiment with Electricity*, above the fireplace.

3

THE ILE DE FRANCE

The Ile de France is the ancient, poetic, but still very current name for the region around Paris which has for more than a thousand years been the theater of great events in French history and culture. The capital is close at hand, and yet life is very different here, in big old houses half-hidden in bosky gardens. Step inside: a timeless air reigns over the polished furniture, the vast kitchens, the sun-faded fabrics, the chairs that invite one to conversation, and the dining rooms redolent of large Sunday dinners with all the family. These houses always have an attic and a cellar, armoires full of linen, and closets crammed with memories of the past. Above all, they have that luxurious commodity of which city-dwellers dream, space: corners, landings, corridors, store-rooms – all those areas that would now be dismissed as "waste" space. The rooms exude a sense of wellbeing, and you can almost smell the beeswax polish and the woodsmoke. Houses like this make you want to read Balzac, turn over the pages of albums filled with sepia photographs, take up jam-making, watercolor painting or petit-point; or just sit and dream. Even when new owners have completely transformed a house with fresh paint, brand-new curtains and restored furniture, there is still the sense of a bygone sweetness, which is the essence of the Ile de France.

A still-life of easy living, set against a many-paned window
typical of old houses in the Ile de France (see p. 142).

LIKE AN ISLAND IN A GARDEN SEA

A Directoire house, set in a lush green garden. The countryside is on the doorstep, and Paris only moments away by the autoroute. It is the sort of place that would convert the most committed city-dweller to rural life – and indeed its owners, although they work in the city, live here all year round. What joy to escape from noise, pollution and traffic jams to the tranquil *atmosphere of these rooms, furnished with the help of Alain Gaucher, a designer who is also a friend. Here children and visitors are welcome to join in and take pot luck, to help themselves to flowers from the garden, to practice Chopin or Debussy on the piano, to read in the shade of old trees, and to be convinced that they are living on an island in the midst of a green sea of leaves.*

Above: The house is a splash of white in the green, like the swans on the river or the doves that flutter among the trees.

Opposite: In the dining room the table is covered with an antique patchwork quilt and surrounded by cheerful red leather chairs.

An anteroom (*left*) opens directly onto the garden, and leads through to the dining room. "Allegretto" is the mood of a musical corner of the living room (*opposite*) – a perfect spot for a "a little day music."

The summer living room, in soft shades of ochre, almond green and pale blue, opens onto the terrace. The poetic mood of the house is summed up in the chaise longue – perfect for daydreaming – the birdcage and the baskets of flowers.

FANTASY ON A COUNTRY AIR

Falling in love or moving house can happen for the most unexpected reasons . . . "Two washhouses and five springs [on the estate] made me decide to buy the shell of the house. The garden is my passion and my inspiration, and I walk in it every day." These pastoral sentiments come from the well-known decorator Yves Taralon, a designer of fabrics and of major international exhibitions: though he is thoroughly Parisian, he now lives and works sixty kilometers from the capital. When he found it the house was a burned out ruin; he transformed it into an idyllic country retreat where poetry and comfort are perfectly balanced, full of inventive ideas, and rich with the spirit of France. Of course, he denies that any of this has been "designed." His professional skill comes through in the handling of volume and the management of space, but basically the house is an expression of the things he loves: friendship, good food, gaiety and simplicity – the things that matter in life.

Eye-catching simplicity: flowers and glass-chimneyed candlesticks on a stone ledge; garden chairs, tilted inward at the end of the day; and the white-shuttered house seen across the garden in spring.

Opposite: A corner of the terrace. You can almost smell the roses after rain.

Above: The laundries on the estate no longer echo to the bustle of washerwomen. This one has become a haven for the reader in search of quiet, the dreamer in search of solitude.

Special touches in the dining room include the slipcovering of alternate chairs to give variety and the use of a starched white tablecloth over a patterned one. On the table, basil plants in china pots scent the air more deliciously than any potpourri.

Right: The relaxed atmosphere of the living room is created from a host of imaginative details – wheat, green and growing, in an old stone mortar next to the 1820s fireplace; a 19th-century *torchère* in Pompeian style; the faded look of the paint on the walls, which takes skill to achieve; the friendly old-fashioned armchairs freshly slipcovered for summer; and the intriguing plaster tables, made by John Dickinson in the late 1970s.

Left: The vista through from the dining room to a distant drawing room is almost palace-like. There are no doors between the rooms, creating an airy spaciousness; the "corridor" is paved with unpolished terracotta tiles.

Opposite: More than a pantry and less than a dining room, this pastel space is used for breakfast and for arranging flowers. Marbling in blue paint adds a touch of glamor to the simple pine buffet.

Opposite and below: Yves Taralon's bedroom is suffused with terracotta tones. The tan leather and chrome chair strikes a contemporary note, while the little cluster of things around the desk betrays the designer's pet interests – objects from Japan, photographs of the Palais de Chaillot in Paris, and flowers from the garden.

Right: In the study, hung with fabric from Alsace, there are large mahogany bookcases and a vast desk of light-colored wood. The lamp, here as elsewhere, is made from an antique candlestick.

HARMONICS

Henri Garelli, known as a maestro of design, likes to think in musical terms. His golden rule is, "In every interior design scheme there must be, as it were, a harmonic progression." In this Palladian villa he has orchestrated styles and colors like a musician composing a symphony. Starting with the reception rooms, marked "allegro con fuoco," and passing on to the bedrooms, to be played "andante," the movements succeed one another and lead up to the "finale con brio" – a lavish swimming pool. This decorative score is written in a major key and played without a single false note, leaving the audience relaxed and delighted.

In a composition conceived by the landscapist Alain Fey (*below*) a checkerboard of stone and grass leads the eye back to a teak bench framed by timber uprights and a swing. The garden in front of the pedimented house (*right*) is worthy of Vuillard.

One whole wall of the library/smoking room is lined with a 19th-century glass-fronted bookcase. The Paisley pattern upholstery fabric echoes the colors of the Savonnerie carpet.

Comfort comes first in the living room, where table and chairs are of
light mahogany. The soberly striped sofas display a riot of cushions
covered with exuberant Second Empire fabrics.

In the dining room, the keynote is the warm color of walnut. The 18th-century French table is veneered with burr walnut. Of walnut, too, are the English 19th-century chairs and the Directoire console table. And the wall paneling seems to be walnut again – but this time it is wood-graining in paint. On the table no placemats are used; note the solid color dishes under the dinner plates, and the mixture of silver and silver-gilt cutlery.

Left: The guest bedroom. The walnut twin beds are 19th-century, the bergère 18th-century. The oval window is covered by a ruched blind.

Below: The master bedroom, seen through an English mahogany screen. The walls are covered with a Louis XVI style fabric; the bed is late 18th-century, and the pale sycamore chaise longue is Biedermeier.

The bathroom is typical of Henri Garelli's refined mastery of the mixing of genres. A 19th-century copper bathtub is set into an alcove, below an English glazed triptych. A Restauration petit-point carpet and stool, and a Napoleon III shaving stand of silvered metal, complete the effect of old-fashioned charm.

Tea in the garden, in a delightful summerhouse of stripped wood that the designer found in another garden. In this bower, already beginning to be covered with roses, the atmosphere is of an idyllic past, evoking the novels of E. M. Forster or Edith Wharton.

HARMONY, FRENCH STYLE

If one had to choose a single example of French provincial style for posterity, or to convey the essence of French decorative taste to the outside world, this house near Paris would have to be it. Its ideal size, its rooms arranged in enfilade, its oeil-de-boeuf windows, its many-paned glass doors, its beamed ceilings and its stone floors, all unite to express provincial douceur de vivre. *The house has belonged to the same family since time immemorial, and constant use has kept it young.*

What of its decoration? It is not really right to call it decoration. Better to say, atmosphere, for no professional interior designer or architect has been at work here: it was the mistress of the house herself who chose the light colors and the position of the furniture. The overall arrangement was dictated by the classic proportions of the rooms. The effect is of warmth and measured calm. If one had to preserve a single image of French harmony . . .

The garden front of the house. A gravel walk surrounds the lawn, where two spherically trimmed box trees stand guard. The shutters are white against the all-enveloping Virginia creeper.

Opposite: A gallery on the ground floor links the living room and dining room and serves as a little reading room. In the background is a glass-fronted cabinet containing the family's finest pieces of antique silver.

The entrance hall. The buffet covered in mirror glass, below the large mirror on the right, is a particularly ingenious product of the late 19th-century cabinetmaker's art.

Right: The luminous dining room has French doors leading to the garden and to the entrance hall. Note how the cream paint and the stone flagged floor link the two spaces.

A 19th-century bronze is placed below an 18th-century drawing in its original frame with masked corners.

Left: In the living room opening off the gallery an 18th-century sofa and armchairs stand on traditional parquet flooring. The different shades of cream of the walls, ceiling and upholstery create a unified interior.

Above: One corner of the living room has a fireplace tucked under the stairs leading to an upper gallery. Note the Louis XV cabriolet chairs upholstered in leather and the chair with slender colonnettes typical of the Louis XVI period.

Opposite: A detail of the entrance hall, where a large Dutch oil painting hangs above a Louis XVI semicircular table. Antique earthenware candlesticks and a bowl filled with potpourri add a lively touch.

Opposite
Above: The games room at one end of the house leads directly to the garden, and is made to seem part of it by Ramuntcho de Saint-Amand's mural painting. *Below left:* In spring and summer the pantry is used for flower arranging. *Below right:* An African pot becomes a vase to be filled with tea roses.

Right: Everywhere the refined taste of the owner is discreetly present: a casual glimpse of a turning on the stairs reveals a green 1930s vase placed next to a celadon green door.

A WISE FOLLY

A country house, set in a pretty garden: every Parisian's dream. But what do people do when they inherit a house that is neither a cottage nor a castle but a sort of folly, built at the end of the last century in the style of Marie Antoinette's beloved Trianon? They keep it, of course, were it only for the formal French garden that surrounds it, with its avenues of linden trees and conifers, its groves and its bowers, and the aura of exquisite luxury that owning such a park confers today. And, while they have the paintwork renewed, and modernize certain essential conveniences, they determine to preserve the atmosphere of the place as they found it, neither updating it nor making it into a 19th-century pastiche. So we should not look here for any of the sophisticated conceits of the professional interior designer. There may be a little less furniture, but otherwise the house must look much as it did when it was first built. The life style of its new owners, and the laughter and games of their children, have made it young again, while at the same time it retains the mellow feeling of a bygone age.

Above: A classical statue in the depths of the park, worthy of celebration by a Romantic poet.

Opposite: The house rises at the end of a formal avenue, a folly built on the ruins of a priory demolished at the Revolution.

One of the bedrooms. The collection of furniture seems haphazard, as so often in old country houses; and yet the Louis XVI beds, the Napoleon III oil lamps and the turn-of-the-century rattan furniture all live happily together.

Right: The dining room is redolent of past glories, with a marble console table below a painting by a follower of Poussin, a 19th-century English portrait, and an antique Chinese carpet in delicate and unusual colors.

A sitting room is arranged as a winter garden, around an original fountain that is still in working order. *Opposite:* The symmetrical columns suggested the choice and placing of the furniture, which includes a daybed, Napoleon III chairs with buttoned upholstery, and a Louis XIV console table. *Right:* The same room, seen from the entrance hall. The only concession to modern taste is the use of wicker cachepots.

THE HOUSE OF FLOWERS

Some country houses are so elegant that they look like apartments in town. Others are so rustic that they look like parodies of country inns. This one takes its cue, appropriately enough, from the surrounding garden, and effortlessly succeeds in being what a real country house should be. It has white shutters, a covering of Virginia creeper, a smooth lawn and a few fruit trees, and above all a profusion of flowers – in flowerbeds, compositions, bouquets, drawings, printed fabrics and papers – both out-of-doors and in every room. For Patrick Lavoix, the owner, who is a fashion designer for Lanvin Hommes, is obsessed with flowers. He photographs them, season by season, to record their colors, and he has made them the decorative theme of his house. In the bedrooms they appear, unobtrusively, in the fabrics of the beds, drapes, and armchairs. In the dining room you will find them on the chairs – and blossoming on the chandelier. In the salon they bloom in profusion on seats and lampshades, screens and ottomans, window blinds and tables, and, as in the garden, their colors and shapes intermingle with a freedom that is utterly natural.

Above: At one end of the house, an awning like those used in Italian markets creates a shady terrace on the lawn.

Opposite: Lunch under a cherry tree, outside the vine-clad house. Light folding chairs have been repainted to match the white iron table.

The art of indoor gardening: there are more than fifteen different kinds of flower in the living room, but the dazzling mixture of colors is offset by the rough stone of the walls and the soft green of the carpet. Two ideas to remember are the books tucked in above the window on the right, and the low table made up of an iron balcony and a sheet of plate glass.

Opposite
Top: In a bedroom up under the roof the boldness of the exposed stonework contrasts with the refinement of the Oriental rug and framed prints.
Below left: The patterned border of the dining room drapes forms an introduction, in blue, to the owner's love of flowers.
Below right: On the stairs, a traditional rope serves as a guide up the steps polished by time and wear.

Right: An eclectic corner of the flower-strewn living room: below a Japanese screen, an 18th-century Italian armchair upholstered with chintz nudges a Chinese porcelain stool.

Left: A corner of the living room. On the wall is an 18th-century Italian overmantel; below it, two Japanese Imari ware vases converted into lamps stand on a mahogany buffet stamped with the maker's name and date – Jansen, 1925. The fruitwood chairs are upholstered with the same glazed chintz that is used for the drapes.

Below and opposite: A rhapsody in blue and white sings through the dining room. The early 18th-century painted chairs are upholstered with a floral pattern in blue. The painted metal chandelier sprouts porcelain blooms, and its lampshades match the upholstery fabric (which is also used for a tablecloth when the table is laid for dinner). On and above the mantelshelf, a collection of blue-and-white tin-glazed earthenware.

4

THE WEST

Once upon a time, in Western France, there were three houses. One was in a town, somewhere in Brittany. Another stood by the sea on an island in the Atlantic. The third was in the depths of the country on the border of Normandy. The first, elegantly urban in a little walled garden, was completely redecorated for an enthusiast by two designers, and radiates warmth and intimacy. The second was transformed by its present owner into a holiday house fit for children and grandchildren, who would feel at home in its friendly atmosphere, surrounded by country furniture and faded chintz. The third was originally a farm, and most of its features were retained by the famous painter who lives there year-round with his wife and children; its simple furniture, handsome country-made objects, light colors, and closeness to nature give it a character that is unique. Town, beach, country: three houses, three ways of life. They cannot speak for the whole of the West, but they unmistakably proclaim themselves "made in France."

A room in a Breton town house, for a connoisseur of interior design (see p. 152). The scrolly table came from a butcher's shop.

A PASSION FOR DESIGN

Each room is a distinctive stage set, each object cast in a particular role. Since you can't collect houses, the real enthusiast for interior design collects different styles of *decoration. This old house, newly restored with the help of the Breton designer Maurice Savinal, serves as a backdrop for his stylistic dramas.*

Opposite: A play revolving around the meeting of ancient and modern. Among the ancients are tazzas made of serpentine, marble newelpost balls, a Louis XVI mirror and an 18th-century mantelpiece. Among the moderns, a Moroccan wool carpet, a low table of metal and glass, and a stool by Mies van der Rohe. Occupying neutral ground between them are folding screens covered with marbled paper.

Right: A wicker chair from the Philippines, a bust of one of Napoleon's marshals, and an 18th-century Italian dog of carved wood animate a landing on the stairs.

The sitting room with a 19th-century flavor is organized around a fireplace topped with a plain sheet of mirror glass. Gouaches of Naples hang above the Empire sofa. The marble floor is covered with rush matting. The low table is made up of a mahogany column drum and a granite slab. A group of 1930s stoneware vases gleam under the light beside the fireplace, while on the mantel stand faience figurines from Dinan in Brittany.

BETWEEN WIND AND TIDE

This island in the Atlantic with its temperate climate, its unique light and its wonderful ever-changing sky has its devotees, fanatics who would not trade its salty landscape for all the palm trees in the world. Some thirty years ago, a Parisian fell head over heels in love with the place, and bought some old abandoned buildings that had formerly been used by oyster farmers. Where there had been nothing but drained marshland she created a garden, and restored the five little houses to make a magical holiday refuge for her children and grandchildren. Each room, filled with country furniture and family possessions, is a snug haven – but every window gives a glimpse of the nearby sea and the long rows of oyster beds left exposed as the tide creeps out.

Above: A vestibule between living room and bedrooms. On the left is a fall-front desk made on the island in the 18th century; on the right, a dresser from the area, transformed to hold a collection of books about the sea.

Opposite: A corner of the living room, with its open timber roof. The walls are of thinly plastered stone, the floor of waxed brick. The 18th-century stone mantelpiece was discovered on the island, in a shepherd's hut.

In the spaces that now form the living room wines and spirits were stored and oysters were collected for shipping. Old sea-chests and a loom are reminders of the lives of local fishermen and their wives in bygone days. A glass-fronted *bonnetière* in the background (*left*) displays local faience. In one corner of the room (*above*) an old well was retained: it is twenty meters from the sea, and fills with salt water every time the tide comes in.

A stone-paved path
extends from the living
room out into the
garden, and also gives
access to three separate
little guest houses.

A new patio was created around a pool. Its arcades, copied from
those of the square beside the village church, give it the look – and
the tranquillity – of a cloister.

OVER THE FIELDS
AND FAR AWAY

A peaceful, ancient farm set in the middle of a vast plain: that is what appealed to Yves Lévêque, who as a painter draws his inspiration from landscape and unbounded space. The golden color of the surrounding wheatfields guided his wife Martyn in her decoration of the rooms. The owners' respect for natural materials, their love of simple forms, and their easy hospitality give the house a special character, where nature and man live in intelligent harmony.

The buildings, which were the farm of a Louis XIII chateau, are of flint and clay with brick at key points of the structure, and have their 17th-century tile roofs. A goose stands in one of the dormers – a folk art carving placed there by the owners with a wink at the surrounding countryside.

Above left and right: Martyn Lévêque is a keen collector of antique samplers in cross-stitch. One is displayed in a vestibule, behind a woodcarver's masterwork; others hang in a little dining room, where the lamp base, of glass filled with water, was originally used by a lacemaker.

Above and opposite: Yves Lévêque's studio, at one end of the house, is covered by a great timber roof, and filled with light and silence.

Above: A large canvas by Yves Lévêque entitled *The Hen* broods over the living room. The decorative objects include antique balls for the bowling game of *pétanque*, and a weathervane propped up casually in a corner.

Opposite: In the entrance hall, as golden as a harvest field, the visitor is greeted by an 18th-century *tribulum*, a rasp-like board drawn by horses to thresh grain.

In the bedroom too there are samplers, objects made of wood, and country furniture. Note the fiber matting on the floor, the color of ripe wheat.

The vast kitchen, with its original beamed ceiling, serves as a dining room and as a laboratory, where Martyn Lévêque tries out delicious local recipes.

5

THE SOUTH-WEST AND THE BORDEAUX REGION

As in all regions where grapes are grown and good food is prized, here life seems sweet and the welcome warm. In Toulouse or Bordeaux, Agen or Pau, hospitality is a law, conviviality a virtue, and fine cooking a duty. The houses are as varied as the landscape: on the same trip you might come across a massive medieval castle, an exquisite 18th-century charterhouse, a Neo-Classical gentleman's seat, or a later 19th-century worthy's dwelling. Their decoration is as eclectic and as carefully thought-out as a local menu, where an invigorating omelette aux cèpes *may follow exquisite* pâté de foie gras. *You will find pompons, braid and buttoned upholstery that evoke lush, snug, 19th-century interiors; a chateau with grand rooms and provincial furniture of the time of Louis XVI; the home of a collector, where furniture and objects are arranged with subtle symmetry; an old family house where each successive generation seems to have added a wing, altered a staircase or remodeled a room. Throughout the different styles, a single art prevails – the art of living. If you ask one of these fortunate owners to give you his recipe for successful decoration, he will probably say, one part tradition, one part comfort, and one part personal taste.*

The recipe, it seems, is foolproof . . .

A chateau sympathetically restored for a lover of old stone (see p. 172).

A MEDIEVAL CHATEAU BROUGHT BACK TO LIFE

Is it possible to restore youth and beauty to a chateau of which the oldest parts go back to the Middle Ages and the youngest to the 18th century? The present owners fell in love with the building, and determined to do just that. It took years of work and patience, but the result was a triumphant success – a success due to their perfectionism and taste. Perfectionism, as they ensured that when any materials had to be replaced, such as beams, flooring or woodwork, the replacements were either authentic features salvaged from elsewhere or faithful reproductions made by local craftsmen, and that traditional techniques were used in their installation. Taste, as they created a particularly subtle mixture of old and new that delights the eye and enhances the quality of life, antique provincial furniture blending happily with cool modernity to produce a truly lived-in feel. The result of this conjugation of past and present? Pluperfect.

Opposite: Turrets with "Genoese" roofs cling to the corners of the house. The austerity of the walls is offset by the shutters, painted a gray-blue that is distinctive to the area.

Right: Loose hangings of heavy ecru linen soften the exposed stonework of the entrance hall.

The spacious, simple, country kitchen. The terracotta floor tiles, restored open timber ceiling, and rustic bench give it a traditional air. A sophisticated note is struck by the Dutch brass chandelier, its gleam echoed in the row of copper pans.

Opposite: The bedroom of the mistress of the house has an 18th-century flavor, with its mantelpiece of painted wood, overmantel, mirror, screen and fruitwood secretaire. The Cogolin carpet is modern.

Right: A happy marriage of old and new. A Louis XVI bed and an antique chair from Southern France are matched with a modern painting by Jean-Louis Germain.

ATMOSPHERE ...

Are we in 1870 or a hundred years later? Is this one of those interiors lovingly recorded by painters in the second half of the 19th century, or the modern home of people with a flair for comfort and style? The near-perfection of Jean-Louis Riccardi's designs makes the question almost impossible to *answer. Here at La Grave Bechade, a chateau in the Bordeaux region, Riccardi used all his imagination to recreate the muffled, exquisite atmosphere of a bygone age. But his choice of fabrics, the way he mixes printed patterns, and his placing of furniture are lessons for any genre.*

The use of two main colors, darkish red and sky blue, gives the living room a distinctive air, while the unusual combination of different prints based on roses and broad stripes, for curtains, walls, carpet and upholstery, pushes distinction to the point of daring. Balancing this profusion is the symmetrical placing of twin lamps, sofas, armchairs and corner cupboards.

Blue and red appear again in the dining room – blue for the wall coverings and curtains of printed moire and the velvet of the chairs, red for the bergère. Both colors tone in with the mahogany furniture, the walnut paneling, and the patterned carpet by Jean-Louis Riccardi. In his choice of objects, the designer gave free reign to that feeling that drives us to hunt around in junk shops for exciting finds: the table is Louis XVI, the chairs are 19th-century and American, the brass chandelier is of the 1880s, and the terracotta statues, raised to the right height on simple cubic bases, date from the 18th century.

PASSION'S FRUITS

To come upon this hidden place is a magical experience. Imagine, at the end of a garden of studied naturalness, an elegantly simple house. There is an Italianate quality to its façade that speaks of the South. Within, you are in the domain of a man of culture and humor, the favorite retreat of a painter in love with color and flowers. In this house with a long history, built in the reigns of Louis XIII, Louis XIV and Louis XV and then partly restored in the 19th century (as was so often done in the cause of "progress"), the furniture too comes from different periods, and feels like a family collection acquired over the centuries. It sets the tone, but remains in the background: for here objects rule. Objects of all kinds! Animalier bronzes, terracotta putti, cups made of agate and other semiprecious stones, prints, drawings, skilfully framed sketches in red chalk, curiously shaped boxes, unusual candlesticks, grouped into spontaneous compositions by the hand of an artist, ornament the rooms. Potted plants proliferate. There are tapestry-covered cushions by the dozen. But the style of living cultivated by the master of this house is unique; and the warmth of his welcome a rare thing.

The present façade and the cast-iron balustrade date from the 19th century, but the stairs with their double flight were built in the early 18th century on early 17th-century foundations.

Opposite: In the living room on the ground floor three new round-headed arches were created, echoing the form of the windows, so that daylight now comes in from both sides. The space beyond the arches is like an orangery, sheltering plants in the winter.

In the living room, white ornamental plasterwork and old-gold picture frames (*opposite*) set off the Tuscan color of the walls. An interesting feature is the symmetrical hanging of drawings and prints on either side of the fireplace. On the mantelpiece (*above*), a 19th-century copy of Giambologna's *Rape of the Sabines* is grouped with a blue-and-white china cachepot below a Louis XV gilt bronze sconce, in one of those subtle juxtapositions of styles for which the owner has a special flair.

184

Even the garden is that of a collector . . . An Italian bust overlooks the pool in the inner courtyard (*below*), against a background of aromatic plants in pots, Italian fashion; and a cast-iron mask (*opposite*) decorates a mossy fountain filled with papyrus and other water-loving plants.

FROM
ANOTHER
CENTURY

The second half of the 19th century was an age of comfort and profusion, when private life was raised to the level of art. Its style of interior decoration was long despised in favor of severer forms, but now its decoration and architecture are fashionable again. One of its most passionate supporters is the designer Robert d'Ario. Among his works is this house in Toulouse, where he used fabrics and carpets specially copied from historic models, and indulged his love of antiques and authentic period detail. Behind these dazzling wonders lies every convenience that the late 20th century could desire.

The house (*above*) is classical in form, and its doors and windows are surrounded, in Toulouse fashion, with bricks as rosy as the tiles of the roof. Not far away is a pergola (*right*), arranged like a conservatory with plants in large terracotta pots and climbing shrubs. The curly cane furniture and carpet are modern. The fine wooden screens have the delightful effect of a veil through which one glimpses a lush green world.

Two strong details that sum up the style of the house and Robert d'Ario's love of Second Empire modes of decoration. *Opposite:* The use of the same fabric wallcovering in the entrance hall and the informal sitting room creates a layered effect. The curly pediment over the door is contemporary with the Neo-Gothic chair. *Right:* The same pattern continues up the stairs and covers a little chair on the landing. The wall surface is further enriched by a collection of 19th-century German watercolors, extended to an infinite vista in the mirror.

The living room upstairs has a central free-standing fireplace. Over the hearth (*above left*) is an arch-topped mirror, echoed by another mirror at the far end of the room. On the other side are a display cabinet and a mirror framed in fabric. Note the harmonious use of shades of dark red and reddish-purple, and the toning screen which cleverly enlivens a flat wall.

A bedroom centering on a great fourposter bed hung with a Napoleon III style fabric.

The bathroom includes three intriguing features: the big 1880s mirror hung above the handbasin, which is built into a corner; the paneled bathtub, given grandeur by two lacquered wooden columns; and the simple roller blind decorated with an antique painted panel.

Opposite: The same striped fabric boldly covers walls, Louis XVI armchairs and the tester of the iron bedstead, copied from an 18th-century model.

THE PRIVATE REALM

How is one to reconcile formal living, active sport, and private life, when all three have the same setting? The perfect answer was found by Pierre and Florence Tari, whose business obliged them to reside in the vast chateau of Giscours in the Bordeaux region, which had been acquired by his family in the 1950s as the center of a vineyard known since the days of Louis XIV. "Château Giscours" is now world-famous, and this fame has brought with it a host of obligations, including receptions attended by three generations of the Tari family. The chateau itself proved inadequate, and a wing was added

where Pierre and Florence Tari live with their children. This less formal area is a real family home, designed for living rather than for show. Each room has its own natural style – a combination of living room and library devised for reading and for conversation, a veranda that is itself an airy living room, cheerful bedrooms, and a friendly old-fashioned kitchen. Here and there are mementos associated with polo – for polo (like the wine business) takes Pierre Tari and his sons all over the world; but they always return, covered with glory, to the peace and intimate warmth of Giscours.

Part of Giscours was built in Neo-Renaissance style (*above*) to welcome the Empress Eugénie on her trips to and from the resort town of Biarritz. Then, in a late 20th-century gesture that took its cue from the 19th century's willingness to mix styles, a long veranda was added to one side (*opposite*), where summer reigns all year round.

Left: Inside the veranda – an exotic world of tropical plants and Asian bamboo furniture.

Below: The Taris' favorite corner of the garden, beside an artificial lake surrounded by ancient trees.

The kitchen is a
delicious mixture of
different ingredients.
The chairs in early
16th-century style and
the early 20th-century
chandelier might almost
be amusing finds from
a junk shop; the wall
tiles were made at Apt
in Provence; and the
idea of masonry niches
for storage is Mexican.

A bedroom in the chateau, updated to the 1980s. A miller's ladder leads to the clothes closet on the upper level; beyond is an ultra-modern bathroom.

An eclectic interior with a wonderful sense of unity. Scarcely any two things in this little family living room are of the same date or origin. There are low Napoleon III chairs covered with tapestry and a Régence bergère upholstered in a plain pale fabric; a 19th-century painted tin tray on an English mahogany folding support and a modern table made of wood and glass; an Orientalist painting over the fireplace and a collection of 1930s objects; and on the floor a patchwork of rugs from different regions of the Middle East.

The real living room at Giscours is the library with its surrounding gallery. The shelves, of elm, contain not only books but a special section of international magazines, and polo photographs and prizes. There are hunting trophies from far-off lands, and, as elsewhere in the house, a richly eclectic blend of furniture and objects.

ON THE FRINGE OF THE 19th CENTURY

Two designers from Bordeaux, Jean-François Braconnier and Christophe Larquey, applied all their skill to restore a mansion in the old quarter of Bordeaux to the appearance it might have had in the later 19th century, with antique furniture and objets d'art placed in an authentic setting. A brilliant stylistic exercise, this: chairs with buttoned upholstery, fabrics trimmed with *fringe and braid, little occasional tables, patterned carpets, paintings, stained glass, rubber plants – not a tassel or a leaf is missing. In the ornately decorated suite of three rooms that forms the heart of the house, we wander – amazed, intrigued, and delighted – in the great age of bourgeois opulence.*

The central space, which is living room, bedroom and library all in one, has the snug atmosphere of a 19th-century smoking room. Key elements are the antique carpet of embroidered felt, the comfortable fireside chair covered with old fabric, the fringed ottoman, the 1870s Minton vase poised on a wooden column, and the portrait (by Jacques Leman) of a man whom we might well take for the master of the house.

Opposite: The salon, a classical 18th-century-style room such as you find in all Second Empire interiors. The ornate gilt furniture is Italian, of the third quarter of the 19th century.

The living room/bedroom/library is separated from the winter garden by blue drapes, which herald the shift from warm artificial light to cool daylight. The 1830s Austrian bed, the Biedermeier chair drawn up to a writing table suitably covered with baize, the Minton majolica vases, the folding screen decorated with landscape scenes, and even the elaborate moldings of the ceiling all conspire to create the sort of interior that was fashionable in the late 19th century not only in France but in Central Europe and England as well.

The 19th century had a special passion for winter gardens. This one was devised around a stained glass panel by the famous glass-painter Caranze. Points to note: the matching pair of upholstered armchairs, authentic right down to their elaborate fringe and tassels, the divan with its cording and braid, and the modern carpet with a 19th-century flavor to its stripes, by Madeleine Castaing. Something to remember is how the green of the potted plants adds intensity to the turquoise tones that are used in the room.

6

THE SOUTH

It almost seems eccentric to speak of interior design in connection with Provence, for what strikes one most here is out-of-doors. First of all, the light: brilliantly clear on windy days, bluish-white in the heat, purple at dawn, rosy-gold at sunset. Then there are the scents: of aromatic herbs, cedar, figleaves, bay trees in bloom, lavender, and hot stone. There are sudden glimpses of a village perched on the top of a mountain, of ocher-colored or chalky earth, the poetic faded blue of the shutters of a shepherd's hut, the geometry of little dry-stone walls, the great open landscapes leading in the far distance to the gleam of the sea or the dark shadow of mountains. Finally, there are the houses — simple farms or proud fortified dwellings, narrow in villages and spreading broadly in the country under great tiled roofs. What are they like inside? Designed for coolness in summer and to resist the piercing mistral wind in winter, they have floors paved with stone or brick, and walls usually painted white or a shade of sienna; brightly glazed green and yellow pots glow in the kitchens, and meals are eaten off antique plates from Apt or Vallauris. The key to Provençal life is the radassier, *an ample rush-seated bench, which irresistibly invites one to that indolent repose known in the language of another land of the sun as "dolce far niente."*

Antique dishes of tin-glazed earthenware from Apt
stamp this dining room "Provence" (see p. 224).

COLLECTIONS RULE

*He paints, she writes, they collect – laurels,
objets d'art, and houses, of which this one,
set in the landscape of the Var region, is the
latest of almost twenty. Bernard and
Annabel Buffet had lived for a time in
Normandy before finding this chateau in
Provence, which was not only beautiful and
in an idyllic setting but vast. For the Buffets
need a lot of space. Bernard's studio, his
fiercely guarded domain, takes up a third of
the area. The rest is the kingdom of their
collections – of animalier bronzes, ostrich
eggs, silver, liturgical objects and examples
of hardstone – which Annabel has enthroned
with a flair equal to her enthusiasm.*

The chateau of Tourtour, in that secret,
unspoiled Provence which still exists inland from
the denatured coast and the crowded beaches,
was built in the 17th and 18th centuries and
restored in the 1930s. As is traditional, the south
front is shaded by big old plane trees, and in the
terraced garden fountains and springs cool the air
and refresh the spirits with their trickle and
splash.

In the living room, the visitor is greeted by a portrait of the mistress of the house, painted by the master (*left*). Early pieces of furniture in dark wood and 19th-century sofas covered with stamped velvet play a discreet supporting role to Bernard Buffet's paintings. An 18th-century bronze of the infant Hercules stands on the marble table in the foreground. Elsewhere in the living room (*below left*), a painting by Buffet of a church hangs above a medieval statue of the Virgin in polychromed wood; on either side are bronze figures of animals by Rosa and Isidore Bonheur.

Opposite: A 19th-century circular mahogany table gives another glimpse of the collections that enliven the house, among them an Empire statuette, cloisonné enamel vases, and tortoise shells.

The kitchen/dining room, approached from a little sitting room with white slipcovered chairs (*opposite*), offers an appetizing mixture of simplicity and sophistication. The 19th-century mahogany furniture is English. On the walls, above the tiling, are plates with the arms of the city of Nancy, made by Gallé, and antique pots of Moustiers faience. A recess serves to display 18th-century French and English silver. The gilt bronze and opaline hanging lamp introduces an ornate note of luxury.

FOR LOVE OF
THE VINE

The Lubéron is known as a cultivated region. Writers, directors, musicians and intellectuals in all fields choose to come here in their moments of freedom. And what is actually cultivated there? Fruit, lavender, and the occasional grapevine. The most recently established vineyard is that of Val Joannis: the estate, created a few years ago by a wealthy buinessman, includes a handsome bastide which was restored and decorated by his wife. Their house, like their wine, has the qualities that age well.

A wrought-iron gate leads into the courtyard of the house, which is paved with river pebbles like the old threshing-floors in the region. The table is laid in the shade of an immense *micocoulier* or African lotus tree, a Provençal relative of the elm.

The garden, created with the help of the landscape designer Loup de Viane, is full of secret corners and surprises, like this door (*left*), framed in scented chervil and jasmine and flanked by two big Italian pots filled with verbena. The olive tree, the oleander in a tub, and the lavender and flowering sage in generous beds (*opposite*) are all children of the sun. The ground is covered with fine gravel, a further Mediterranean touch.

Right: The entrance hall feels unmistakably like Provence, with its terracotta tiles and painted chest of drawers made in the region in the 18th century.

Below: The master bedroom. Fabric copied from a historic model was chosen for upholstery, drapes and tablecloth to harmonize with the Provençal quilt on the bed; on the floor, an 18th-century Savonnerie carpet. *Right:* Another Provençal quilt, covering a table on a landing.

Above and above right: Two views of the bathroom/boudoir, hung with a traditional Provençal patterned fabric; traditional too is the *radassier* or daybed. Note the marbled bath, the petit-point carpet (from a church) on the terracotta-tiled floor, and the 18th-century English hanging shelves.

Opposite: The dining room. The flowered slipcovers of the chairs consort happily with the antique Chantilly dinner service and the simple lettuce-green cotton damask tablecloth. The taste of the mistress of the house is once again shown to be faultless.

A SILK FARM TRANSFORMED

Like several other houses in this part of Provence, this 17th-century complex was originally a silk farm. The designer Françoise de Pfyffer transformed it into a holiday house, adding to its comfort without diminishing its character, making it more modern but scarcely less authentic in feeling. The rooms used to house the silkworms became the drawing room, dining room and kitchen, the attics became bedrooms, and the big lean-to sheltering the well became a vast gallery/

living room linking what had originally been two separate buildings. The furnishings are sober. A few dark pieces of country furniture, local pottery and glass, and the use on beams and shutters of a blue like that of the copper sulfate dusted on the nearby vineyards – so much for the region. A few bold modern works of art, a few handsome antiques – so much for decoration from elsewhere. Under the matchless light of Provence, the two worlds live very comfortably together.

Holidays, happiness, sun and the South . . . From a window, the view is like a Cézanne. Below is a terrace, covered with gravel in the Mediterranean way, with a table sheltered by a wisteria-clad pergola.

The gallery/living room, lit by an immense window, houses the old well, on which stand a bouquet in the colors of sunshine and a sculpture by Arman. The chaise longue is 18th-century, as is the carved lion. The Greek carpet is modern.

An entrance hall, at one end of the building. The ceiling, with its alternation of exposed beams and plaster, is typical of old houses in Provence. The straw hats on the table come from every quarter of the globe.

The gallery. The ceiling
beams are painted
yellow and the walls are
whitewashed; the floor
is paved with stone
from Ménerbes. Set
against this simplicity
are a large canvas by
Philippe Leroy and an
ancestor portrait, a
piano with a stool by
Diego Giacometti and
(looking at a glance like
a tray of drinks) a
paper sculpture by
Pavlos.

Top: In a bedroom, dazzling white was chosen for the painted floor, the plain linen curtains, the bedspread of Provençal cotton lace and the stone bedside tables.

Above: The dining room table is lit by an antique hanging lamp from a store. The dishes on the right-hand wall are antique tin-glazed earthenware from Apt (see also p. 211). The drapes and the squab cushions on the chairs are made of blue-and-white-striped mattress ticking.

Right: A cozy drawing room, designed with autumn days in mind. Note the low table by Diego Giacometti, the sculpture by Christo on the mantelpiece, and, on the walls, a work by César and a drawing by Paul Rotterdam.

METAMORPHOSIS AT MOUGINS

When it was discovered by Patrick and Jo Frémontier, two antique dealers from Cannes, this house at Mougins was like countless others – a low pink-washed rectangle, vaguely Provençal in flavor, with a fine view of the sea. Now, heightened by one story, broadened by two wings, pierced with large windows, accented by dark lines, rejuvenated, one might even say styled, it is definitely one-of-a-kind. If you look very hard you might discern an influence from Rome, something of Scandinavia, even perhaps a whiff of California.

Certainly it provides every pleasure imaginable in a handsome, sophisticated, Mediterranean house.

The façade covered with dark green trellising looks as though it had been drawn with a pen. The story added above the roof terrace contains an extra bedroom.

Top: A living room entering the garden, or how to use a modern bay window. The opulent cushioned stools came from an old mansion on the Riviera.

Above: A spot for a siesta, under an awning by the swimming pool. Note the lawn, where a pattern is formed from squares of grass and slabs of stone, and the panels of trellis work that symbolically shelter the pool from the house.

Above: The walls of the living room, painted stone color, enclose a collection of objects of diverse provenance – Etruscan vases on the mantelpiece, an inlaid marble table top which began life as part of a floor in a palace in Naples, Roman antiquities, and a 17th-century allegorical painting of Hercules.

Opposite: The entrance door is flanked by columns bearing Neo-Classical urns. On the table is a curious commemorative model from America.

ACKNOWLEDGMENTS

This book could never have been realized without the very generous cooperation of the owners who allowed us into their houses and apartments: to them I extend my warmest thanks. My gratitude goes too to the *Maison & Jardin* team, and in particular to Christine Grange-Bary, Lisa Roussel, Françoise de Valence and Aude de La Conté. Finally I am also indebted, for their help, to Jean-Marie Baron, Nanou Billault, Marie-Claire Blanckaert, Sonia Dieudonné, Jean-Louis Gaillemin, Marie-Jo de Loisne, Claudine Mulard and Florence Trocmé.

Daphné de Saint Sauveur

From darkness to dazzling light, in the secret garden of an old farm in Provence.

REFERENCES AND CREDITS

The picture stories from which the present book has been designed appeared originally in *Maison & Jardin*. The list that follows gives the title of each article, the date of publication, and the name of the photographer.

p.1
"Les dimanches de Victor Laloux"
February 1987
Jacques Bachmann

p.2
"Le XIXe en toute intimité"
February 1987
Jacques Bachmann

p.6
"Les dimanches de Victor Laloux"
see above, p.1

p.11
"70 m² de candeur et de naturel"
see below, pp. 28–31

pp.12–17
"Les feux de l'automne"
October 1987
Roland Beaufre

pp.18–21
"Le petit théâtre de la vie"
October 1987
Roland Beaufre

pp.22–7
"Un réveil en beauté"
October 1987
Pascal Chevallier

pp.28–31
"70 m² de candeur et de naturel"
October 1986
Jacques Bachmann

pp.32–7
"Chez une jeune femme rangée"
April 1987
Roland Beaufre

pp.38–41
"Un passé très présent"
September 1985
Jacques Primois

pp.42–7
"Le style Plaine Monceau"
December 1985/January 1986
Pascal Hinous

pp.48–55
"A Jacques Grange, lettre de château"
October 1985
François Halard

p.57
"Le goût du bien-être"
February 1986
Pascal Chevallier

pp.58–63
"Couleur de bonheur"
February 1988
Pascal Chevallier

pp.64–9
"Le show des choses"
March 1987
Roland Beaufre

pp.70–73
"L'âme voyageuse: un avant-goût de romanesque"
September 1987
Roland Beaufre

INDEX OF NAMES